...AND ONE SLICE WITH ANCHOVIES!

...AND ONE SLICE WITH ANCHOVIES!

A **CRANKSHAFT**® collection

by Tom Batiuk and Chuck Ayers

Andrews and McMeel
A Universal Press Syndicate Company
Kansas City

ISBN: 0-8362-1707-1

Library of Congress Catalog Card Number: 92-75351

JEFF! COME HERE...QUICK!

LOOK... ISN'T THAT CUTE?

MINDY'S HELPING DAD PUT IN THE GARDEN!

HERE, GWAMPA! I GOTS ALL THE BEANS YOU DWOPPED!

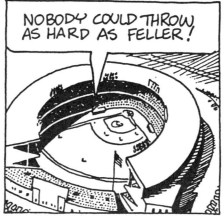

17

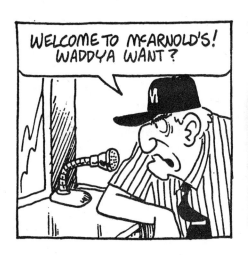

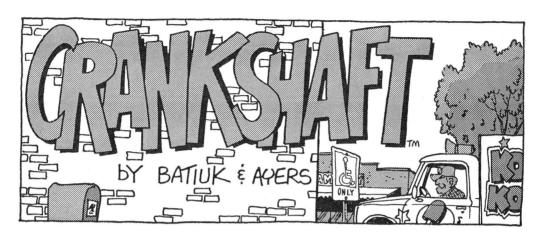

INCREDIBLE! TWELVE WINDOWS IN THIS BANK AND ONLY THREE ARE OPEN!

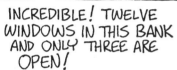

THE ONLY TIME THERE WAS A TELLER IN EVERY WINDOW WAS WHEN THEY TOOK THE PICTURE FOR THE STOCKHOLDERS BROCHURE!

HOW COME YOU ONLY HAVE THREE TELLER'S WINDOWS OPEN WHEN THE BANK ACROSS THE STREET HAS **SIX** TELLERS!

THAT'S IMPOSSIBLE!

THE BANK ACROSS THE STREET ONLY HAS THREE WINDOWS!

THEY WERE **TWO** DEEP!

I TOLD DAD IT WAS RIDICULOUS TO BE DRIVING THAT SCHOOL BUS ALL AROUND...

AND I THINK I FINALLY CONVINCED HIM TO GO OUT AND GET SOMETHING A LITTLE SMALLER.

VROOOM!

@#☆❀❊≋ ROWDY OLD FOLKS!!

Lemonade

DAD JUST TOOK OFF ON HIS MOTORCYCLE TO SEE GRACE.

I DON'T KNOW...HOPEFULLY **SHE** CAN TALK SOME SENSE INTO HIM ABOUT RIDING THAT THING.

OH BOY!

THE COUNTY FAIR!

HOLD IT! BEFORE YOU TWO GO RUNNING OFF....

WE'LL MEET AT THE ENTRANCE TO THE FAIRGROUNDS IN TWO HOURS! GOT IT?

GOT IT, GRAMPS!

OKAY... HERE'S A QUARTER! GO HAVE SOME FUN!

I CAN REMEMBER WALKING UPTOWN IN THE EVENING....

AND EVERYBODY WOULD BE SITTING OUT ON THEIR PORCHES WITH THEIR RADIOS ON.

AMOS N' ANDY USED TO BE ON ABOUT THIS TIME IN THE SUMMER, AND YOU COULD HEAR IT AS YOU PASSED EACH HOUSE ON THE STREET.

IN FACT, YOU USED TO BE ABLE TO WALK CLEAR INTO TOWN LISTENING TO THE RADIO THE WHOLE WAY.

I KNOW WHAT YOU'RE GOING TO SAY AND IT'S NOT THE SAME....

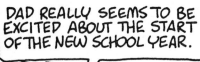

IT'S PRETTY EASY TO SPOT THE MOTHER OF A KINDERGARTNER WHO'S GOING OFF TO SCHOOL FOR THE FIRST TIME....

THEY ALL HAVE ANXIOUS LOOKS WITH TEARS WELLING UP IN THEIR EYES...

AND THEN THERE ARE THE MOTHERS OF THE OLDER KIDS....

THANK YOU SO MUCH FOR LETTING ME COME ON THE BUS TO TAKE PICTURES!

NO PROBLEM!

I'LL EVEN LET HER COME BACK TOMORROW TO TRY IT WITH THE LENS CAP OFF!

42

CRANKSHAFT ™
BY BATIUK & AYERS

LOOK AT THAT! THREE MOTHERS RUNNING NECK AND NECK AFTER THE BUS WITH STUFF THEIR KIDS FORGOT!

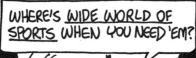

WHERE'S _WIDE WORLD OF SPORTS_ WHEN YOU NEED 'EM?

I THINK EVERYTHING WENT PRETTY SMOOTHLY FOR THE FIRST WEEK....

WITH SPECIAL CONGRATULATIONS TO ED CRANKSHAFT...

WHO HAD FORTY-TWO CARS BEHIND HIS BUS ON TUESDAY....

FOR A NEW OPENING DAY RECORD!

ALL RIGHT!

WAY TO GO, ED!

THAT CRANKSHAFT! WHAT A PRO!

HE ALWAYS PARKS AT THE FAR END OF THE LOT SO THE KIDS HAVE TO WALK FARTHER.

DID YOU HEAR THAT CRANKSHAFT HAD A KID SUSPENDED YESTERDAY?

NO KIDDING!

DID IT DO ANY GOOD?

WE'RE STILL NOT SURE....,

HELP!

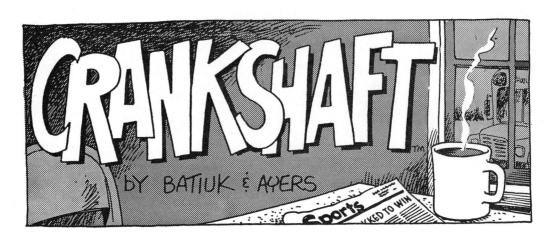

BOY, ON THESE COLD FALL MORNINGS, THERE'S NOTHING LIKE A GOOD CUP OF COFFEE!

I'LL SAY! ANYONE KNOW WHERE I CAN GET ONE?

CRANKSHAFT! THERE'S AN ANGRY MOTHER ON THE PHONE SAYING YOU LEFT HER KID BEHIND!

NO DOUBT ABOUT IT.... OL' CRANKSHAFT IS THE BUS DRIVER'S BUS DRIVER!

HE'S HAD SO MANY KIDS MISS THE BUS OVER THE YEARS....

THAT THE PARENTS ON HIS ROUTE GET AN AUTOMATIC REBATE ON THEIR TAXES!

WE CAN'T GET TOGETHER TOMORROW NIGHT, ED, BECAUSE I'VE VOLUNTEERED TO TEACH A CLASS FOR ILLITERATE ADULTS AT THE LIBRARY.

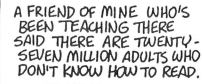

A FRIEND OF MINE WHO'S BEEN TEACHING THERE SAID THERE ARE TWENTY-SEVEN MILLION ADULTS WHO DON'T KNOW HOW TO READ.

SOUNDS LIKE A PRETTY BIG CLASS!

SO WHY ARE YOU GOING TO TEACH ILLITERATE ADULTS HOW TO READ ANYWAY?

WHY?

WELL, FOR ONE THING, LITERATE ADULTS ALREADY KNOW HOW!

VERY FUNNY!

ED! WHAT A NICE SURPRISE... BUT I REALLY CAN'T TALK NOW... MY STUDENT FOR THE READING COURSE IS GOING TO BE HERE ANY....

YOU!?

YOU'VE ALREADY WASTED THREE MINUTES...!

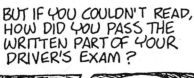

BUT IF YOU COULDN'T READ, HOW DID YOU PASS THE WRITTEN PART OF YOUR DRIVER'S EXAM?

EASY... I JUST HAD SOMEONE READ ME ALL THE QUESTIONS AND I MEMORIZED THEM!

AMAZING!

WHAT'S SO AMAZING? I'M NOT STUPID..... I JUST CAN'T READ!

ED, IS THERE A SPECIAL BOOK THAT YOU'D LIKE TO LEARN TO READ?

GWAMPA, WILL YOU READ MY FAVORITE STORY?

YEAH, THIS ONE!

'THE CAT IN THE HAT'!?

SO SUE ME! I HAPPEN TO LIKE ANIMAL STORIES!

AND NO ONE ELSE REALIZED THE REASON YOU WOULDN'T READ TO YOUR GRAND-DAUGHTER WAS BECAUSE YOU COULDN'T?

NAW, I'D JUST ALWAYS MAKE UP A DUMB EXCUSE OF SOME KIND!

NO! HOW DO YOU EXPECT TO LEARN TO READ IF I'M READING TO YOU ALL OF THE TIME!?

WHAT'S THE ONE DOLLAR SERVICE CHARGE FOR?

THAT'S A PASSBOOK WITHDRAWAL CHARGE.

YOU MEAN YOU'RE GOING TO CHARGE ME A FEE FOR MAKING A WITHDRAWAL FROM MY **OWN** SAVINGS ACCOUNT?!

IS THERE ANY CHARGE FOR BREATHING THE AIR IN YOUR BANK!?

DON'T BE SILLY...

YOUR FIRST FIVE CUBIC FEET ARE FREE!

OH, DAD... IF I'D ONLY KNOWN THAT YOU COULDN'T READ BEFORE THIS... THAT'S WHY YOU'D NEVER READ BEDTIME STORIES TO MAX AND MINDY...

AND WHY EVERY CHRISTMAS WHEN I ASKED IF YOU WANTED TO ADDRESS SOME CHRISTMAS CARDS TO YOUR FRIENDS YOU'D ALWAYS SAY..."CHRISTMAS CARDS ARE TOO EXPENSIVE AND A WASTE OF TIME!" AND HERE IT WAS BECAUSE YOU COULDN'T READ AND WRITE!

NAW, IT WAS BECAUSE CHRISTMAS CARDS ARE TOO EXPENSIVE AND A WASTE OF TIME!

.... AND SO I USED TO SIT AROUND WITH A NEWSPAPER OR A MAGAZINE AND GO THROUGH THE MOTIONS JUST TO BE LIKE EVERYONE ELSE IN THE FAMILY.

FINALLY, I JUST DECIDED THAT I WASN'T GOING TO LET STUPID PRIDE KEEP ME FROM LEARNING HOW TO READ.

FUNNY HOW THAT WORKS, ISN'T IT...? BECAUSE I'VE NEVER BEEN PROUDER OF YOU!

EH....

JUST THINK WHAT IT'S GOING TO BE LIKE ONCE YOU'VE LEARNED HOW TO READ, DAD!

THERE'S A WHOLE NEW WORLD THAT'S GOING TO OPEN UP FOR YOU!

YEAH, BUT NOW I SUPPOSE I'LL HAVE TO BUY READING GLASSES...

DON'T SWEAT IT! YOUR FIRST PAIR IS ON ME!

IT'S REALLY BLOWING OUT THERE!

ON THESE OCTOBER NIGHTS, WITH THE RAIN AND SLEET COMING DOWN....

IT'S GREAT TO GET INDOORS....

SNUGGLE UNDER A WARM AFGHAN....

AND WATCH THE WORLD SERIES!

58

THERE'S NOTHING QUITE LIKE THE AROMA OF A BUS FULL OF DAMP ELEMENTARY KIDS!

ARE THERE ANY PROBLEMS YOU WANT TO MENTION?

YOU BET! YOU'RE AN HOUR AND A HALF BEHIND ON APPOINTMENTS...YOU NEVER SEE THE SAME DOCTOR TWICE HERE...THE MAGAZINES IN YOUR WAITING ROOM ARE ALL TEN YEARS OLD...

WHAT CAN YA DO FOR BACK PAIN?

WELL...

HOW ABOUT THIS?

AHHHH!

I THINK THAT FALL IS MY FAVORITE SEASON OF ALL!

YEP... I'VE SEEN A LOT OF AUTUMNS COME AND GO IN MY TIME.

EVERY NOW AND THEN I STOP AND WONDER IF THIS IS THE LAST AUTUMN THAT I'LL EVER SEE....

OH, DAD! DON'T SAY THAT!

I DON'T EVEN WANT YOU TO THINK ABOUT SOMETHING THAT AWFUL!!

WHAT'S THE BIG DEAL? LOTS OF FOLKS MY AGE MOVE TO FLORIDA!

WHAT CAN I BE FOR HALLOWEEN, GRAMPS?

I WANT TO GO AS SOMETHING REALLY FRIGHTENING!

HOW ABOUT A PRESIDENTIAL CANDIDATE?

I SURE HOPE WE GET SOMETHING DIFFERENT FROM CRANKSHAFT THIS YEAR!

LAST YEAR HE GAVE OUT LITTLE PACKETS OF METAMUCIL!

TRICK OR TREAT!!!

EH, ALL RIGHT...

I'LL TAKE THE TREATS!

CRANKSHAFT

BY BATIUK & AYERS

ADULT READING LESSONS

WHATCHA DOIN', GRAMPS?

I'M WORKING ON MY READING LESSON.

IF YOU DIDN'T KNOW HOW TO READ, GRAMPS...

WHY DID YOU GET A NEWSPAPER ALL THESE YEARS?

WHUMP!

FOR THE EXERCISE!

68

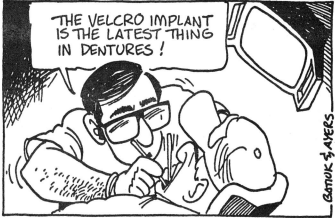

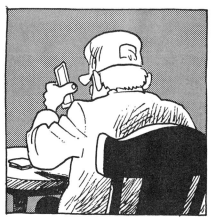

YOU KNOW, IN A LOT OF WAYS, DAD HAS STILL MANAGED TO RETAIN A LOT OF CHILDLIKE QUALITIES!

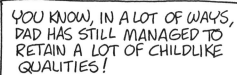

EVEN THOUGH HE'S OLD, HE SEEMS TO REMEMBER WHAT IT'S LIKE TO BE A KID!

IN A WAY, HE'S FOUND THE SECRET TO ETERNAL YOUTH!

YEAH, ARRESTED DEVELOPMENT!

AHEM!

YOU SHOULD DO SOMETHING ABOUT THAT COUGH!

WHAT'S THE PROBLEM? I PAID YOU!

IT'S CUSTOMARY IN THE CIVILIZED WORLD TO GIVE A LITTLE BONUS AT THE HOLIDAY TIME TO THOSE WHO TOIL IN YOUR SERVICE THROUGHOUT THE YEAR.

EH, ALL RIGHT.... HERE'S A QUARTER.

OH GOODY! I CAN GO TO COLLEGE NOW!

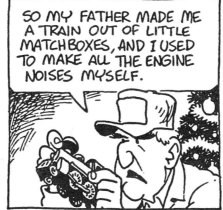

THERE'S NOTHING BETTER THAN A CRACKLING FIRE ON A COLD SUNDAY AFTERNOON!

I CAN'T THINK OF WHAT ELSE YOU COULD POSSIBLY WANT...

EXCEPT FOR MAYBE A FIREPLACE.....

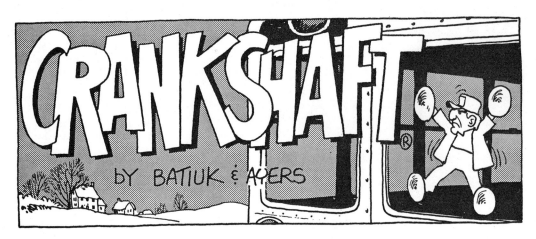

SHOOT! THIS OLD SEVENTY-EIGHT WAS MY ONLY COPY OF GERSHWIN'S RHAPSODY IN BLUE!

WELL, I'LL JUST GO OUT AND BUY ANOTHER COPY! HOW DIFFICULT CAN THAT BE?

DO YOU SELL RECORDS HERE?

RECORDS?

YEAH, THEY'RE ROUND, BLACK AND HAVE A HOLE IN THE MIDDLE!

YOU KNOW, I THINK I SAW SOME OF THOSE IN A BOX IN THE BACK ROOM!

THE LITTLE JOHNSON GIRL IS STILL BACK THERE RUNNING AFTER THE BUS!

I WAS SURE I'D LOSE HER GOING THROUGH THE HIGH WATER AREA!

EH, IT LOOKS LIKE THE LITTLE JOHNSON GIRL IS YELLING SOMETHING.

I'M NOT GONNA GIVE UP UNTIL I CATCH YOU, CRANKSHAFT!

I DON'T KNOW THE MEANING OF THE WORD QUIT!

WELL, THAT'S WHY YOU'RE GOING TO SCHOOL!

CRANKSHAFT
④! BY BATIUK & AYERS

REALLY!

I'M NOT MAKING IT UP!

NO KIDDING! WHO'S YOUR BUS DRIVER, ANYWAY?

CRANKSHAFT!

THAT FIGURES!

SO LET ME MAKE SURE I'VE GOT THIS STRAIGHT....

YOU'RE TELLING ME THAT **YOUR** BUS DRIVERS DON'T **CHARGE** YOU ANYTHING TO RIDE TO SCHOOL?

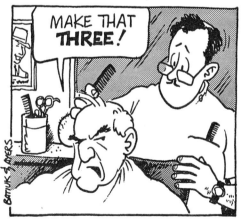